STRUCK
BY A LIGHTNING BOLT

J'LYN A. BRADFORD

Copyright © 2020 by J'Lyn A. Bradford

This is a work of fiction. Names, characters, places, and incidents either are the product of the author's imagination or are used fictitiously. Any resemblance to actual persons, living or dead, events or locales is entirely coincidental.

Text copyright 2020 by J'Lyn A. Bradford
Front cover illustrated© 2020 UKALA SHAHID

All rights reserved. Published in the United States by The Thread, LLC
Library of Congress Cataloging-in-Publication Data
Publisher: Thread, LLC, The (June 24, 2020)
Language: English
ISBN-10: 1733296670
ISBN-13: 978-1733296670

Name: J'Lyn A. Bradford
Bradford, J'Lyn A., Author
Title: Struck by a Lightning Bolt

Description: Four teenagers playing basketball. They see a lightning bolt. They are not bothered by it at first. Then the lightning comes very close. One of the boys is struck by a bolt, but this isn't ordinary lightning. The lightning takes the boy, and he's stuck in a strange world. His friends are confused because they don't know if he has super powers, or if he has run away, or the unthinkable—is he dead?

No part of this publication may be reproduced, distributed, or transmitted in any form or by any means, including photocopying, recording, or other electronic or mechanical methods, without the prior written permission of the publisher, except in the case of brief quotations embodied in critical reviews and certain other noncommercial uses permitted by copyright law. For permission requests, write to the publisher, addressed "Attention: Permissions Coordinator," at the address below.

leonie@leoniemattison.com

For my parents,
who made me write this book!

DEDICATION

To the kids my age who were diagnosed with ADHD and are feeling like their life doesn't matter. You matter!
You are more than enough!

ABOUT THE AUTHOR

J'Lyn A. Bradford is a middle school teen, animal and sports lover, and author. She was diagnosed with ADHD at a very early age, but that did not stop her from thriving. From taking care of her pets to combing her hair, cooking for her family, and more, J'Lyn knows how to work with and evolve beyond her diagnosis—ADHD does not hold her back or define her! J'Lyn is here to give her support and encouragement for others who may be struggling with their identity. And show them ways to uncover and build inner strength.

TABLE OF CONTENTS

Prologue 1

It All Began When I Met Bryan... 5

The Supercell 16

Stay Brave 27

Zapped by Lightning 38

The Search 48

The Eye of the Storm 58

Epilogue 68

PROLOGUE

Arilyn always had a hard time not laughing when she caught me lounging in the hammock catching a few zees in the park with my mouth wide open. I'm a pro at finding the perfect way to spend a nice afternoon, and I wasn't moving for anyone.

"Jay, tell me!"

Arilyn's voice startled me out of my thoughts. I sighed and looked up at the tree above me, running my fingers through my hair. It was a perfect September evening for hammocking in Central Park. Arilyn was sitting to my left, watching the locals stroll around the park grounds. My dark skin had soaked in the sun all afternoon, and the evening breeze was cool and refreshing.

"Come on, Jay," Arilyn pleaded. She was becoming impatient, but that's just how she is: nosy and impatient. I hate that she always wants to know everything about me! I mean, I love Arilyn. She's been my favorite cousin ever since I can remember, but she just won't let go. I shouldn't blame her, though; it's my fault that she's even curious in the first place. I let slip one little detail of my crazy, unbelievable summer, and now she won't leave me alone.

"Jay, I know there's more to the story. You can't hide this from me!"

"Yes I can, actually," I said, sticking my tongue out at her. "You wouldn't believe me anyway."

"Oh, cut the excuses! No one's going to believe you if you never tell anyone," Arilyn yelled. She was never afraid of causing a scene or attracting the attention of nearby strangers. Sometimes it really seemed like she couldn't care less about where she was or who could hear her.

I opened my mouth to answer but stopped myself. Arilyn had a point: if I never gave people anything to consider, they wouldn't even have a chance to believe me. But the story is utterly ludicrous! There's no way anyone could believe that my friend got struck by lighting and disappeared for four days.

"Helloooo??" Arilyn said. "Earth to Jay."

This time I wasn't daydreaming. I was just ignoring her.

"Alright—I'll tell you." As soon as the words left my mouth, I wished I could take them back, but there was no turning back anymore. I took a deep breath. "Arilyn, what I'm about to tell you is going to sound like a stupid, completely made up story. But it's not a nightmare or some bizarre tale all in my head. What I'm about to tell you is one hundred percent true."

Arilyn nodded and stopped smiling. She matched my grim look and serious tone.

I cleared my throat and tried to prepare myself. Although this story had a happy ending, it wasn't going to be easy to share the details of it. What we experienced was horrible, borderline frightening. I had never told anyone what happened at the beginning of the summer. I intended to, but I just didn't know how, when, or with whom I would share it. And no less have them believe me!

"Earlier this year, my friend Bryan was struck by lightning."

CHAPTER 1:

IT ALL BEGAN WHEN I MET BRYAN...

It all began when I met Bryan earlier in the school year. He had just moved to our area after his parents had a rough divorce. He wound up with his dad, and they moved from New Jersey all the way to California. I'd always liked making friends with the new kids around the block, but Bryan became more than just the new kid at our school. He became one of my best friends.

I never really thought Bryan was any cuter than the other boys at school, but there was just something about him. I liked how he built others up instead of tearing them down. I liked his cornball jokes and silly faces. I liked how he was friendly to everyone, especially the people who got pushed to the side and ignored. He really was just an ordinary-looking boy, but his heart was beautiful.

We had lots in common, so we became friends really quickly. We liked the same videogames and sports, so we had lots to talk about. He was also pretty good at basketball, and that's what I liked about him most of all. We would have lunch together and talk about our favorite teams or why I think LeBron James is totally overrated. Bryan doesn't agree, but I know I'm right and am bent on convincing him, even if it takes a whole week of lunchtime discussions. Lucas, Anniyah, and I were especially happy that he was a fan of basketball because that meant we could finally play pick up, two on two games with someone competent. Most of the other kids we'd played with could barely dribble a ball.

Becoming friends with Bryan was easy, but getting to know him was a whole other story. He was just so dense! Sometimes I would catch him staring at me in class, and when I would smile back at him to be nice, he suddenly fell silent or just mouthed "what?" as if he were supposed to say something! I always wondered why he couldn't catch my drift that I was just being nice to him. One day I was just trying to be friendly, and he started teasing me with a really irritating nickname he gave me: "bun muffin top." To make matters worse, I had a new hairdo and although he noticed it, he would avoid eye contact with me. One time, he ran in the opposite direction when he saw me coming down the hallway. It was as if he'd seen a ghost. Sometime I would catch him crying, and one time I saw him talking to himself, but it was if there was an invisible person talking back to him. He even reached out his arms as if he was hugging someone. I swore I even saw tears streaming down his face. When I asked him what was going on, he ran away and didn't show up again until the next day. He didn't seem to get that we were his friends and that we were not there to hurt him. Even Anniyah and Lucas could tell that something was off.

After the four of us had been having lunch together for a week or two, I finally plucked up the courage to ask Bryan to play basketball with us after school.

"Hey Bryan," I said, my voice cracking. I was trying really hard to seem relaxed, but my nerves got the better of me. I'd always get anxious around him. "I, uh, would you want to   um, we were thinking—"

Lucas cut me off. I just couldn't spit it out. "She wants to know if you wanna play a few pick-up games with us after school at the Y."

"Oh, sure." Bryan smiled and turned to look at me. "Why didn't you just ask?"

My face turned bright pink, my palms were sweaty, and I sheepishly smiled, not knowing what to say. I put my head down in shame and attempted to get up and just walk away to avoid feeling embarrassed. Thankfully, the bell rang, ending lunch before my stillness got too awkward. I quickly got up and silently thanked the bell for saving me from an awkward moment with Bryan. I wished he could just be more open with me. Maybe then I could have a normal conversation with him and not feel so nervous. He was completely oblivious and probably just thought that my nervous laugh was super weird.

I thought maybe Bryan was acting a bit weird because he transferred schools towards the end of the year. I had to do that a few years ago and kind of hated it, but when I asked Bryan about it, he didn't seem to mind. I just wished I could connect with him on a different level, but he was definitely hiding something. He had a story to tell, but it was hidden by the mask he wore every day.

Even though we'd only known Bryan for a few months, he'd become pretty close to me and the gang. At this point, Lucas was basically his rival. Sometimes when Anniyah and I were done playing basketball, the boys would go head-to-head while we sat on the sidelines watching. Bryan usually won, but Lucas would call him a cheater and challenge him again. They teased each other a lot while they played and tried to make fools of each other by breaking their ankles or faking them out.

I really enjoyed watching Bryan play Basketball Sometimes he'd catch me staring, and I'd quickly look away. I kind of wanted him to notice me the way I noticed him. I'd only known him for a few months, and I was already so intrigued by who this mystery boy was. I thought that maybe he just didn't like me. Maybe he just didn't trust me enough to talk to me on a more personal level. But that didn't stop me from hoping that he'd catch on sooner rather than later.

One day after school, I rode my skateboard to the YMCA with my basketball under my arm to meet up with the gang for our routine pick-up game. My friends were already there waiting for me under the shade of a tree. As I got closer, I caught fragments of a conversation. Anniyah shot me a look that told me I wasn't going to like what I heard. She slowly shook her head back and forth like she was warning me away, but I joined the approached anyway and began to pick up on the conversation between Lucas and Bryan.

Lucas shrugged. "Girls are like that sometimes, dude. Just apologize and move on."

That was all I needed to hear to know that they were probably talking about some girl Bryan liked. I rode up to their spot in the shade and sat down. "What's going on, guys?" I tried to sound nonchalant.

"Bryan didn't call his New Jersey girlfriend last night," Lucas said, drawing out the word "girlfriend" like it was some sort of curse word.

"She's not my girlfriend, Luc," Bryan growled. "And I don't get it. What's the big deal? So what, I didn't call. I wish she would get over it." He frowned and crossed his arms, clearly annoyed with the whole situation.

"Well maybe if you took your big head out of the mud, you would see that she cares about you. That's probably the big deal," I said, throwing my basketball hard at Bryan's stomach.

He tried to deflect it but missed. "Ow! What was that for?" Bryan leaned forward, massaging his lower sternum.

"Oh, I don't know! Probably for the same reason your New Jersey girlfriend is mad at you," I yelled. I just couldn't hide how mad I was.

I really liked Bryan, but sometimes he was just so dense. He could be so carefree that the emotions of the people around him would fly right over his head. He couldn't get it through his thick shell that friends are supposed to be there for each other, but they can't help you if you don't let them.

I got up and grabbed my skateboard with a huff. I left the YMCA without even saying goodbye. I wasn't in the mood for basketball anymore.

That was my first unofficial fight with Bryan. That night as I lay in bed, he texted me and apologized. I ignored him and went to sleep. I really wasn't in the mood for a sappy makeup text. I wasn't even actually mad at him. I was just jealous of the Jersey girl. Maybe that's why he couldn't see that I liked him. Who knows? Maybe my pride was getting in the way. Maybe he did like me, and that's why he didn't call the Jersey girl. I don't know. I wish he would just say what he meant.

School the next day was really awkward. Anniyah, Lucas, Bryan, and I sat together for lunch and our shared classes, but it just wasn't the same. We could all feel the tension between Bryan and I. That day, as lunch ended and Anniyah and Lucas got up, I stuck around for a minute to talk to Bryan alone. He seemed to sense that he should stay.

"Are you okay?" he asked.

"Yeah, I'm fine. Are you?" He could probably see right through me. I was clearly not okay.

Instead of answering my question, he changed the subject. "Would you wanna go—I mean, if you have the time, uh—get ice cream after school with me? Or it can be with other people too! It doesn't have to be just us. Or maybe it could be just us—if that's what you want. Um—or you don't have to if you don't want to…" Bryan trailed off and looked down at his hands. His nervous bumbling was kind of endearing.

I let out a soft laugh and smiled. "Yeah, I would. I'd like that."

Bryan looked up and grinned. "Really!?" I could tell he thought he said that with too much excitement. He regained his composure and tried to act cool. "I mean, yeah. Great. I'll, uh, meet you outside after school."

"Sounds great. See you later." I got up, threw my trash out, and left the lunchroom, surprised by my own nonchalance.

I made my way to class and was surprised to run into Anniyah as I rounded the corner. She'd apparently been waiting for me. She grabbed my arm and pulled me closer to her. "Sooo, what'd he say?" she asked.

Lucas popped out from behind her, also waiting for me to answer.

"Say to what?" I said, as if I had no idea what they were talking about.

"Oh, come on! Don't play common with us. He totally just asked you out!" Lucas said.

"DID NOT!" I suppressed my angry tone. "We're not dating! I just want to be his friend."

"Alright alright it's not a date," Lucas said. "So, what did you guys talk about, then?"

I smiled from ear to ear. "Bryan invited me to go get ice cream after school, so we can get to know each other better."

"AAAHHHH! That's so exciting!" Anniyah hugged me a bit too tightly and shook me a little. Her braids bounced up and down, punctuating her excitement.

I suppressed my giggling and tried to act like it wasn't a big deal, but on the inside, I couldn't wait until the end of the school day. I didn't know what Bryan was hiding, but I was sure that I could find out when we spent some time together. I wanted to help him with whatever it was, and hopefully today would be the day.

CHAPTER 2:

THE SUPERCELL

As soon as the bell rang, I ran to the bathroom to make sure I looked my best. I then called my mom to get permission to go out for ice cream with Bryan. After straightening myself out and double-checking my hair, I grabbed all my things and rushed outside, so I'd be ready when Bryan came.

To my surprise, Bryan was already outside waiting.

"Took you long enough," he teased.

I picked up the pace a little. "Sorry, I was—"

Bryan cut me off. "I was just joking! Don't take me so seriously," he said and smiled.

I smiled back, and we started walking down the sidewalk side by side. Neither of us spoke for a few minutes, and the silence was awful. I didn't know where to start, and I definitely didn't want Bryan to feel like I was prying into his business. I wanted him to talk about himself freely. I wanted him to trust me as a friend.

"So…" I said, trying to pick a starting point. "How's the change to California so far?"

"Well, it's a heck of a lot warmer!" Bryan said, grinning. "I hate how cold New Jersey gets. And I've made some really nice friends so far." He elbowed me to make sure I caught the reference to our little group.

I smiled back at him, glad to know that he considered us friends.

"Do you miss New Jersey at all?"

Bryan paused before answering, mulling the question over. "Sometimes I do. I miss my friends and family, but they call every now and then. My dad said that sometime this summer we might go back to visit." He smiled. "At least I won't be going back during the winter."

I laughed. "That's great! I usually go to New York during the summer to see my cousins in North Manhattan. I spend most of my time with my cousin Arilyn. Her older brother takes us on the subway to Central Park to go skateboarding or hammocking." I glance at Bryan to make sure he's still listening. "I only see Arilyn once a year, so we talk for hours on end trying to catch up on each other's lives."

Bryan nodded. "That's awesome! Actually, I've never been to a big city. I lived a few hours away from a couple major cities in New Jersey, but I've never gone."

I stopped in my tracks and stared at Bryan. "Wait what? You're kidding, right? You've never been to a big city?"

Bryan shook his head. "Nope."

I shook my head in disbelief and continued walking. "Well, New York is super cool. I don't think I'd want to live there, but I love spending time there with my cousins. It's just so different from California."

We chatted about our plans for the summer until we reached our destination: Frank's Ice Cream. We went inside to sit down and get out of the heat. To my surprise, the place was empty. The only person there was the old man tending the counter, and he smiled at us as we walked in.

Bryan hadn't been to Frank's yet, and I was super excited to show him around. What made the place so cool was that it was super old. Frank's has been in Bush, California since World War II. The interior walls and ceilings are decorated with a bunch of old pictures. Bryan ambled up to the counter to order our ice creams, and I took a seat inside one of the fake leather booths. Bryan sat down across from me and handed me a vanilla and chocolate twist cone. Soft serve has always been my favorite.

I took a glance at Bryan's bowl and was taken aback by the strange combination he was eating. "What in the world is under your ice cream?"

Bryan laughed heartily and poked his ice cream with his spoon. "I ordered Italian ice with vanilla ice cream on top."

I scrunched up my face.

"What, you've never seen that before?"

"No! That's ridiculous," I said between laughs. "Who would do that?"

"A lot of people do! This has always been my go to order back home."

I stuck my tongue out and teased him. "Well I guess New Jersey people are strange, huh!"

Our conversation dissolved into laughter, and we continued eating. Every time Bryan raised his spoon to his lips, he looked at me to make sure I could see him wreaking chaos on the world of ice cream law and order. I opened my mouth to tease him again, but a sudden and violent tremor interrupted me. We both grabbed our seats to brace ourselves.

The entire shop shook.

At first, I thought it was an earthquake, but this felt different: there were small shudders and tremors vibrating across the room followed by loud booms that sounded like cannons going off. The sounds were completely overwhelming. At the next boom, I let out a shriek. Dread washed through me. What was going on? What was that horrific noise?

The man working the counter rushed over to our booth to make sure we were alright. Another quake made the room vibrate again. It was so strong and sudden that the man almost fell. Eardrum-busting booms and cracks echoed around us, and they were so loud that we had to press our hands over our ears. My hands barely muffled the destructive sounds echoing outside.

"Get under the table," the man yelled, straining his voice to be heard over the incredible cacophony.

We barely heard him but complied. He joined us on the floor.

I shook with fear. I didn't want to die. I clasped my hands tightly and shut my eyes, saying a silent prayer as the noise grew more intense. I didn't know what to think other than to hope that we'd come out of this alive! I peeked out from under the table and through the window. A few minutes ago, the sun was shining. Now, all I could see was darkness with bright flashes of light dominating the dark clouds. It was as if the sun had been wiped from existence.

"What's going on?" Bryan yelled. I could tell that he was just as nervous as I was, but he was trying to put up a brave front.

"It's a really intense thunderstorm," the man yelled. "You'll have to wait here until it's over."

With our hands firmly pressed over our ears to muffle the noise around us, we sat patiently and waited for the booming chaos to stop. A couple times, I thought it was over and tentatively moved my hands away from my head only to be startled by the thunder. I stopped moving my hands away, even when it was relatively quiet.

The storm lasted over an hour. When the final strike of lightning lit up the sky, the old man stood in the small aisle of his parlor looking out the window. After about five minutes, he finally told us we could leave the shelter of the table. Our ice creams had melted into puddles at that point, but I didn't mind. I'd lost my appetite anyway.

"You better call your parents," the old man said. "I bet they're worried sick about you two!"

I was thankful for the man's kindness and care. He couldn't stop the lightning from striking, but he did what he could to keep us safe. I smiled at him and whispered a quiet thank you.

"Is that how all thunderstorms are in California?" Bryan asked.

"Oh no, that was no ordinary thunderstorm," the old man said, looking grave. "That was a supercell, son."

"A supercell?" Bryan and I asked in unison, glancing at each other for a moment.

"Yeah, a supercell." The old man nodded, thinking. "They're a very intense form of thunderstorms, and they're incredibly rare, especially in this area." The old man paused to catch his breath. He spoke slowly and intently, somehow building tensions in my heart. "I haven't seen one since I was maybe your age. That'd be maybe fifty years ago. If I recall correctly, that was the only supercell ever recorded to take place in Bush, California. They can be incredibly dangerous, so watch out, kids. I saw on the news that they expect multiple storms like this to happen this summer."

"Multiple!?" I felt my eyes bulge and thought they'd fall right out of my head.

"I thought you said you haven't seen one in fifty years!" Bryan said, sounding like he'd caught the man lying.

"I haven't. That's why this is so alarming." The old man shook his head. "I don't mean to scare you kids, but the news also said that the mysterious storm patterns heading our way this summer are like none they've ever seen before."

I swallowed the lump in my throat and turned to look at Bryan. He looked as scared as I felt.

We said goodbye to the man, thanking him for keeping us safe, and left the ice cream shop. As we made our way home, we were shocked by the sight of giant, sturdy trees lying in the middle of the road. Some were horribly burnt, others were still smoldering, and some were completely blackened and sooty. Luckily, only the trees seemed to be damaged. The buildings in that area were untouched. But as soon as Bryan and I walked into our neighborhood, we saw that a tree had been struck by lightning and fell onto a neighbor's roof.

We stopped in our tracks to stare at the poor neighbor's crumbling house.

We silently began walking again until we reached the street corner where we'd part ways to go home. I turned to look at Bryan. "Well, uh, other than the super-cell, I really enjoyed hanging out and getting ice cream together." I tried to keep my tone light and positive, but I was still feeling really shaken up.

"Yeah, me too. I'm really glad none of us were hurt." Bryan paused, chewing on his next words. "You were really brave back there. I'm glad to have had you by my side. I noticed you praying at one point… it was really comforting."

Despite everything, Bryan's quiet words brought a smile to my face as we went our separate ways.

The words brought a smile to my face. We then said our goodbyes and went our separate ways.

CHAPTER 3:

STAY BRAVE

Throughout the next week, all anyone talked about at school was the supercell. I overheard some people talking about raging fires in the forest reserve nearby. Apparently the firefighters were overwhelmed and still struggling to put them out. The dark, menacing smoke of the fire could be seen from miles away. Not only that, but some of the students' homes were victims of fallen trees, like that one house Bryan and I stopped to look at. The lightning strikes were so strong that they left craters all over the roads. They were causing so many car accidents that the town had to close down some of the streets. Some of the craters were so big that the town might not be able to fix them.

It was like the apocalypse had rained down on us. It was all anyone could talk about, but by the end of the week, Lucas, Bryan, and I had heard more than enough. Anniyah, on the other hand, couldn't shut up about it. She liked to be a part of the trends and fads that came her way, and this was no exception.

She held her phone out to me at lunch. "Which picture looks better next to this crater? A or B?"

"Uh, B, I guess?" I said, not really sure there was a difference between the two.

Anniyah squinted at the pictures one last time and nodded. "Okay, good. I thought the same thing. The hashtag #supercell has been blowing up all over Instagram, and everyone is posting selfies with the craters now that everyone's done posting the videos they took."

I couldn't understand how people could treat this as a game. The supercell could have killed people. We were fortunate to be safe and uninjured. But as we saw more footage of the devastating storm, we could see paramedics transporting dead bodies and people who were injured into awaiting ambulances. It was all very frightening and uncertain. Some of the local women were crying, fear and anguish were painted across their husbands' faces as they tried to console them. The look of despair on the kids' faces made me feel sad, and I felt an urge to help others feel better.

"Why do you care about that stuff?" Lucas asked through a mouthful of pizza.

Anniyah rolled her eyes. "Using popular hashtags equals getting more followers. Duh!"

Lucas shrugged. "Well yeah, but why do you care about likes and followers? Why do you care about silly stuff like that?"

"It's not silly!" Anniyah said, clearly offended. "Everyone in school does it. I have the most likes and followers out of anyone else in middle school, and posting pictures with the craters is only going to make my popularity grow!"

"I just don't get it," Lucas said, taking another bite of his food.

Anniyah didn't answer. Instead, she smirked and threw a fruit snack at Lucas, hitting him in the face. He laughed, picked it up, and ate it.

"Well, does social media have anything good to say about the supercell? Any updates or anything?" Bryan asked.

Anniyah grinned. "Ah finally someone who appreciates my cellular expertise." She tapped her screen a couple times. "There've been a bunch of reposts of a few weather forecast clips saying there will be more supercells soon. Their theory is that the next one will take place sometime toward the end of next week."

"Hmmmm-well hopefully we won't be trapped in an ice cream parlor this time!" Bryan smiled at me.

I shrugged and chuckled to myself. We were all trying to make light of a terrifying situation. At the very least, no one was hurt during the first storm, so we should be okay during the next one.

At least, that's what I told myself.

After school, we went to the YMCA to play basketball. We ended up just playing knock out the whole time and goofing off together. After we were tired of playing, Anniyah and I sat in the shade and laughed as we watched the boys try to ride my skateboard while dribbling the ball around. After many attempts, falls, and failure, they finally made a basket. We cheered from the sidelines as Bryan and Lucas high-fived and set up for another shot.

Leading up to the last week of school, we developed a routine. We would go to class, eat lunch together, finish the school day, and head to the Y to hang. We even stopped at one of the craters along the way sometimes. It was knee-deep at the center and about five feet wide. It was so surreal that we lived through the whole ordeal.

Every time we went to investigate the crater on the way to the YMCA, Lucas would say the same thing: "I can't believe a bolt of lightning could make this happen! I mean, it took out a whole slab of the sidewalk, for crying out loud!"

He was right: it was hard to believe that a thunderstorm caused so much damage. I had never seen anything like it. I couldn't imagine just how many potholes and craters would be all over town if this continued to happen. It had been over a week since the last supercell, and they still hadn't been able to fix the hole in the road.

In an effort to keep drama out of my life, I stuck to what I knew. I rode my skateboard, played basketball with my friends, and played videogames. I didn't want to think about the scene at the ice cream parlor anymore. It had infiltrated my dreams and was haunting me. I would dream of the same situation, except that the quakes and storms were strong enough to carry Bryan and me into the sky. After the first nightmare, I woke up screaming. It took my parents a long time to calm me down, but despite their best efforts, the fear of being carried off by the strong wind and disappearing was permanently planted in my head. I told Bryan about my dreams, and he said he'd been having the same fears. I was glad not to be the only one.

On the Sunday before the last week of school, Bryan and I met up to shoot hoops after church.

"We have to be brave," he said.

"What do you mean?" I asked.

"Well, we don't know what's going to happen next. The weather forecast predicted another thunderstorm sometimes this week, and although they think it'll be shorter, it'll probably be just as scary."

I nodded and swooshed another three-pointer. "Yeah. You're right."

Bryan passed the ball back to me, and I paused before taking my next shot. "Have you ever been in a scary situation before?"

Bryan looked at me for a long time before answering. I could tell he was hiding something deep down and debating with himself about whether or not to tell me. "Yeah," he said at length. "I wouldn't say my life has been the easiest."

"How do you deal with things like this?" I was hoping he would give an example of something he'd had to handle. I didn't want him to think I was prying at his secrets or being nosy, but I could tell there was something important he wanted to talk about. He seemed confused about how to say what he meant.

As I waited for an answer, I took another shot but slammed the backboard. Bryan got the rebound and dribbled the ball to the free-throw line to take a turn at shooting.

He sighed. "Well, growing up, I didn't live in a perfect, cookie-cutter home like other kids." Bryan took a shot and seemed to weigh his next words.

I grabbed the rebound and bounced it back to him.

"My mom wasn't the greatest of moms. That's why my dad divorced her. I miss her, but I know this is for the best." He threw the ball at the backboard with all his strength, this time not aiming for the hoop.

I ran after the ball and sat with it on the sideline, beckoning Bryan to sit with me and take a breather. He sat down next to me, and we quietly drank water while Bryan decided what he wanted to say.

"I love my mom, you know? But she couldn't hold a job, and she was drinking a lot, and Dad said we didn't have any other choice. He said we had to leave before things got worse." Bryan sighed. "It was for both our safety and hers."

I nodded solemnly. "I'm really sorry that happened. It must be hard to have a separated family." I paused. "I'm sure you miss her."

"I do." Bryan nodded. "But I know there are greater things for me ahead. I can't let my past define my future." He took a deep breath. "Sometimes I look back and wish that things could change, but I know that I need to be brave during these tough times and persevere. There are people out there who have it worse than I do. I should be thankful for what I have and more forward. We have to be brave." He looked at me. "Just like you were at the ice cream parlor."

I smiled at Bryan. He always knew how to shine a positive light on difficult situations.

"I'm thankful I met you, Bryan. I've learned a lot from you since we became friends."

"I'm glad we met, too." He smiled back at me, and we shared a moment of peace amid the uncertainty surrounding us.

After a few more minutes of relaxing in the shade, Bryan took the ball out of my lap and jogged onto the court to shoot more hoops. I followed him over and rebounded for him, passing the ball back after every shot to let him practice. It almost felt like Bryan getting everything off his chest had helped me more than it had helped him. I realized that he wasn't bottling up his emotions the way I thought he was; he was working through them and looking forward to a brighter future.

That afternoon I decided to try to do the same.

STRUCK

CHAPTER 4:

ZAPPED BY LIGHTNING

The last day of school couldn't have come any sooner. Anniyah, Bryan, Lucas, and I raced to the YMCA as soon as class let out. We always went there because they had the best outdoor courts in town, so naturally, it was our favorite place to hang out. We planned on meeting up during the summer almost as much as we did during the schoolyear.

We started with a quick game of horse to warm up our shots and fool around. After that, it was game time. Our energy level was at its peak because we'd just gotten out of school for summer break, so things got heated really quickly.

"Dude! That's a freaking fowl," Lucas yelled, throwing the ball at Bryan's legs.

Bryan laughed. "Fine, check it at the top. I'll still

beat you," he said with a smirk.

Lucas always complained about Bryan's defense being too close or making too much contact. They'd go head to head with each other every week without fail. Anniyah and I would swap from Lucas or Bryan's team every other game, but I personally liked playing on Bryan's team better. Lucas was kind of a ball hog.

In our time playing together, we each found our unique strengths. Bryan and Lucas were both the best at driving to the basket. They had more brute resilience, making it easy for them to get past anyone guarding them. Anniyah was a nervous player. She was an impressive shooter when she had an open shot, but she didn't play well under pressure. I was the best three-point shooter. I would always linger in the corner, waiting for my teammate to drive. If they didn't get the shot in, they would dish it would to me for an open three.

This game is what led to the incident.

Today's teams were Anniyah and Bryan versus Lucas and me. We were playing first to eleven, and it was game point: Lucas and I were down by one. As Bryan checked the ball to Lucas, a clap of thunder echoed across the sky. I froze, remembering the supercell. We all looked up as it began to drizzle. A thunderstorm was brewing, and we were going to get soaked if we stayed out much longer.

Bryan broke his stare first. "Play on. We're almost done anyway," he said to Lucas.

But I didn't want the game to continue. All I could think about was the old man from the ice cream parlor and how serious he looked when he talked about the next supercell.

Lucas shrugged and began to dribble the ball. I really didn't like the idea of continuing our game, especially considering what happened during the last storm. Another boom of thunder echoed, and I flinched. It wasn't nearly as loud as the supercell thunder, but it was still bringing back terrifying memories and visions of my nightmares. I also didn't want my hair to get frizzy, but I didn't want to take away from everyone else's fun. I jogged to the corner of the three-point line and waited for Lucas to make his move.

He crossed the ball through his legs as he lined up his course of action. He drove to the basket to no avail and passed the ball to me. Another blast of thunder split the sky, and I felt the earth tremble beneath me. I snapped back into the game when I noticed Anniyah running at me to defend. I reacted instantly, faking the shot. She jumped up, reaching for the sky to block in the direction I feigned my shot. I drove left for the open shot to tie up the game.

From the corner of my eye, I saw streaks of lightning strike the top of a building. Bryan was coming towards me fast, and I froze up. As Bryan jumped up to block my shot, the loudest thunder yet reverberated through the sky. Lightning struck the spot directly in front of me where Bryan was. I screamed and dropped the ball, unable to tear my eyes away. The court was filled with a blinding light. I caught only a glimpse of Bryan before he was completely consumed. I could've sworn I was the shadows of his skeleton as the light burst, striking the cement with the force of a grenade.

The explosion of light knocked me onto the ground hard enough for me to scrape the palms of my hands and the backs of my calves. When I looked up at where Bryan should have been, there was nothing. He was gone! I was suddenly out of breath, chest heaving as I swiveled my head left and right looking for him. Anniyah and Lucas seemed just as shocked as I was. What happened to Bryan? Where did he go?

"Bryan?" Anniyah called out, her voice meek and trembling.

I looked at my friends, and they stared back at me through the rain. Loud, ear-shattering explosions of thunder echoed around us, and we covered our ears, but none of us dared to move. We weren't going to leave without figuring out what happened to Bryan.

We stayed out in the rain staring at the spot on the court where our friend had been. There was a large hole just inches from my feet where the lightning had struck. This storm was definitely another supercell, and there were no traces of Bryan anywhere.

Lucas sighed. "Okay—it's not funny anymore. You can come out now," he said loudly, but no one answered.

I got to my feet, looked up and down from the

sky to the court, and evaluated where the lightning had struck. I swallowed the lump in my throat. Was Bryan actually gone? I couldn't be sure. I covered my mouth with my hand to mute my crying as tears trailed down my cheeks.

"Do you—do you really think he's dead, Jay?" Anniyah asked, her voice breaking.

I didn't answer. If I put the thought into words, the moment would feel real. I wasn't sure what to think. I saw the lightning strike him, I saw his shocked face, and the sight of his skeleton was burned into my eyes. I shuddered. There was just no way.

"No." Lucas got up and helped Anniyah to her feet. "Bryan's not dead. He can't be."

"Then where is he, Luc?" I asked, more tears falling from my face.

"I, uh, I—" Lucas stuttered as he tried to think of something to say. "I don't know. But I definitely don't think he's dead. We have to believe. For Bryan."

Both Anniyah and I nodded. I wiped the tears

and rain away and pushed away the horrific thought that my friend might be gone. I wasn't going to jump to conclusions without knowing for sure. I had to believe, not only for Bryan's sake, but also for my own.

"So what do we do?" I couldn't look away from the hole in the court. "No one's going to believe us if we say that Bryan was zapped by lightning and disappeared."

"Maybe we should just wait," Anniyah suggested. "If Bryan's okay, he'll contact us."

I could hear the denial in her voice. She didn't believe anything she was saying.

"What if his phone's fried from the electricity of the lightning bolt? Maybe he can't contact us," Lucas said.

The sky rumbled and flashed again.

"Well, we can't contact him either!" I said. "What options do we have?"

"Do we go to the police? Do we tell anyone?" Anniyah said.

"No!" Lucas and I shouted in unison.

"My parents would kill me if they found out we stayed out in the storm," Lucas yelled, sounding strangled. "They warned me so many times!"

"I say we just wait. If Bryan is alive, maybe he was teleported somewhere else by the lightning." Another loud rumble of thunder interrupted me. "I think we should all just go home. It's too dangerous out here." I glanced at the menacing sky before continuing. "If we just stand around in the rain, the thing that happened to Bryan might happen to us." I ran over to the sideline, grabbed my bag and skateboard, and hurried back to my friends. I took one last look at the crater and spoke with conviction. "We need to be brave."

Flashes of lightning lit up the sky and occasionally hit the ground, but I didn't let it faze me. I was terrified but kept my composure. I had to. It was all I could do to hold onto the thin thread of hope in my heart.

Anniyah and Lucas eventually agreed that we needed to all go home, and we hugged each other. We didn't usually hug, but at this moment, we all needed comfort and some form of closure. We walked out of the Y together and went our separate ways, agreeing to keep the secret to ourselves.

CHAPTER 5:

THE SEARCH

The next morning, I got up early and told Lucas and Anniyah to meet me at the Y as soon as they could. We all rode our boards—skating was the fastest way around town. I rode my skateboard everywhere I went, but Anniyah and Lucas were usually more casual about it. I was the first to arrive, closely followed by Anniyah. When Lucas finally rolled up, we all sat on the asphalt next to the crater in the court. I reached into my bag and pulled out a notebook and pen.

I flipped to an empty page and drew the YMCA court. "Okay so we're here," I said, pointing to my drawing. "This was the last place Bryan was seen. Anyone know what time it was when Bryan was struck?"

"Well, school ended at noon since we didn't have a full day. So it must've been sometime after that," Lucas said uncertainly.

"Oh! I posted a picture on Instagram right before we started playing. Let me see when I uploaded it." Anniyah scanned her phone for a minute before continuing. "Alright so I posted this yesterday at 12:44 PM, so it was probably right around 1 when Bryan, uh…" She trailed off.

"Got it. Bryan disappeared at 1:00 PM." I wrote the time down in my notebook. "Now let's write down a plan of action. I think the first thing we should do is search the town. Nobody heard from Bryan, right?"

"I didn't," Lucas said, scratching his head.

"Neither did I," Anniyah said, sighing.

"Alright you two—let's not get discouraged." I tried to be reassuring. "Who knows, maybe his phone died, or the lightning destroyed it." Neither of them looked hopeful.

"If his phone was destroyed, wouldn't he have been destroyed too?" Lucas said.

"No," I shouted. "Let's not jump to any conclusions. We're going to figure this out. I know Bryan's alive. He has to be. I saw him right before he vanished. He didn't look hurt. He just kind of looked... frozen. And then he warped away." I played back the scene in my head, trying to think of any other details.

"So... you think he warped to somewhere else in the city?" Anniyah asked.

"Well, I don't really know what else to think. Maybe he was struck by one thunderbolt and warped to where the bolt next hit the earth. It's not like this happened all over the place. The storm was only in our area, so that gives me hope that he might still be around."

"I think that sounds plausible," Lucas said, nodding and looking back and forth between me and Anniyah. "I mean, this is all very strange, and I've never seen anything like this before, but I think Jay might be right. Maybe he was just zapped from point A to point B. Who knows? Maybe he just landed down the road."

"What makes you think he's still in the place the lightning zapped him to?" Anniyah asked. She was asking me difficult questions, but I appreciated that she was playing devil's advocate and point out possible flaws in the plan.

"I'm not sure. Maybe he's unconscious? Maybe he doesn't know where in Bush he is. I mean, he is new to this area." I did my best to sound reassuring, but even I was unsure of what to say.

"Well, whatever the case may be, I think Jay's right. We don't know where he is, and we have to get searching while we can." Lukas looked me in the eye, boosting my confidence a little. "Draw up the plans, Jay. Show us where to search."

I smiled at Lucas and jotted little notes and pictures on the map in my notebook. "Okay, so Anniyah, you will start here." I tapped a spot on the map. "Search the area around the local library and make your way back here."

Anniyah nodded

"Lucas, you'll start south of Anniyah, by the school. Work your way back up towards the YMCA."

Lucas nodded.

"I'll start over by Bryan's house on Copper Street. Find out the locations of all the lightning strikes in your designated area. Definitely check those places first in case Bryan really did land in one of those spots. We'll make our way back to the courts at around lunchtime. Keep each other updates in the group chat, and let's make sure to keep each other posted if we find anything.

Anniyah and Lucas nodded again.

"And if we don't find him?" Anniyah asked.

"Let's just pray that we do," I said.

"Is it okay to say I'm scared?" Anniyah's voice shook.

I gave her a hug and softened my voice. "Of course it's okay to be scared. We're going to do out best to find him. We just have to be brave, Anniyah. We're going to get through this."

Lucas put a hand on her shoulder. "Don't worry, Anniyah. Bryan's a fighter and so are we. We'll find him!"

We each hopped on our boards and parted ways. There was no guarantee that we'd find any signs of Bryan, but this plan was our only shot at this point. We had to try.

I stopped at Bryan's house to see if he was there, but no one was home, so I couldn't check. From there, I did a quick Google search for the supercell incident that took place the day before, checking where the lightning strikes had taken place. I found that there were four in my area. I checked each one, calling out Bryan's name as I searched. There were no signs of him being at any of the locations. I felt discouraged and at a loss, but I couldn't give up just yet.

I checked my phone to see if the others had found anything, but I had no new texts. Time had been passing quickly, and it was already time to rendezvous back at the Y, so I got on my board and made my way there.

Lucas and Anniyah were already back at the court, waiting for me.

"Did you find anything?" I yelled as I approached.

"No," Anniyah yelled back. "You?"

I skidded to a stop and sat down on my skateboard. "Nothing." I put my elbows on my knees and rested my head in my hands.

"What do we do now, Jay?" Lucas asked.

I wracked my brain, but I just couldn't come up with a plan B. "I don't really know," I said slowly. "I was hoping that we'd be able to find him."

'Jay, I don't mean to be negative, but what if Bryan—what is he's really gone?" Anniyah said, fear creeping into her voice.

I didn't answer, not wanting to face what seemed to be the reality of the situation.

"Maybe we should tell someone," Lucas said.

"I agree," Anniyah said. "By now, I wouldn't be surprised if Bryan's dad went to the police about his son being missing."

"I don't think he did. Wouldn't he have called out parents first to see if we knew where he was? He knows we're his friends," I said. "And what if we do tell him? What then?"

"I don't know, but I still think we should tell

someone. I'm getting really nervous. I want to believe Bryan's alive and out there somewhere as much as you do, but he literally disappeared," Lucas said, throwing his empty water bottle across the court.

I tried to think of who we could go to, but I already knew that no one would believe us. Even if we managed to convince someone, they'd just search the exact same spots we'd already been to. We sat in silence, each sorting through our own thoughts. I closed my eyes and silently prayed for Bryan to be alive.

We stayed silent for a while, but an idea sparked in my brain. I shot up from my skateboard. "I've got an idea!"

Lucas tilted his head up to look at me. "What is it?" He seemed excited.

"The man at the ice cream shop told me and Bryan that he'd been through a supercell before. Maybe he know something that can help us!"

Anniyah was unconvinced. "You really think we can trust some random old man with our secret?" She rolled her eyes like I was out of my mind.

"He's not just some random old man," I said, exaggerating Anniyah's inflection. "He kept me and Bryan safe at the parlor during the first supercell. We can trust him."

"It's a long shot that he'll know anything, but with no other options, I say we talk to him," Lucas said.

Anniyah sighed. "Fine, but if he can't help us, we're going to Bryan's dad. We have to tell him whether he believes us or not."

I nodded and got back on my board to lead the way to the ice cream parlor.

As Anniyah and Lucas stepped onto their boards, a clap of thunder shook the sky above us. There was no time to waste. We glanced at each other without another word and rode to the parlor as fast as we could. We were hoping to find both shelter and answers.

The darkening sky loomed above us, warning us with an ominous rumble. Another supercell was coming.

CHAPTER 6:

THE EYE OF THE STORM

This storm was even more dangerous and intense than the last two supercells: unforgiving bolts came down from the sky, crashing into the earth. Zaps of electricity triggered rumbling explosions over and over again. Anniyah, Lucas, and I dashed down the sidewalk on our skateboards as the ground quaked beneath our wheels. Another crack came from nearby, followed by a peal of booming thunder that assaulted my eardrums. My heart was racing faster than the lightning all around us. Adrenaline rushed through me, pushing me to ride faster than ever. The short trip from the Y to the parlor felt like it was taking forever, seconds stretching out into years.

Another bolt of lightning struck the ground in front of me. "Watch out," I yelled, swerving around the hole in the sidewalk. I tried to keep my breathing under control. That was such a close call! I could've been hit! Anniyah avoided the hole with a quick turn, and Lucas did an ollie right over it.

Day turned quickly into night as smoke from the fires rose in thick clouds and obscured the sun. The only lights were the streaks of lightning taking over the horizon. The lightning strikes were so close to us that it felt like the storm had a mind of its own. I thought maybe the storm was chasing us down, bent on making us suffer the same fate as Bryan.

After taking the final turn, I spotted Frank's Ice Cream shop—it was open. I skidded to a stop, popped my board into my hands, and ran to the door. It was locked. I yanked on the hands, but the door wouldn't budge. I tried over and over again, hoping that maybe it was just stuck. Thankfully, the old man was just inside and came to unlock the door for us. We rushed into the parlor to escape danger, nearly trampling the poor man as we burst through the entrance.

"Aaah that was so close!" Anniyah said.

"Yeah, it was!" Lucas seemed a bit too excited. "Did you guys see my sick ollie over that hole? Man, did that feel good!"

"No way, dude. I wish I'd seen it!" I said.

We high-fived each other and took deep breaths. We felt like we'd just escaped the grip of death.

The old man locked the door again and turned to look at me. "You again? Why are you kids out there playing in the middle of a dangerous storm?"

Another loud clap of thunder ripped through the sky as if to punctuate his question.

"We actually came to see you, sir," I said in a timid voice.

The man gave me a peculiar look.

"My names Jay, and these are my friends, Lucas and Anniyah."

"You can call me Mr. Debrid. Now, what did you come see me for? I can't imagine you'd ride through a storm just for some ice cream."

I smiled at Mr. Debrid's sense of humor. "I wanted to ask you what you know about the supercells. You said you've experienced one before."

The man sighed and sat down in one of the booths. Anniyah, Lucas, and I followed suit, taking seats across from the man to make sure we could hear him. As he spoke, flashes of lightning and small, rumbling quakes occurred in the background. Despite our fears, we had almost become accustomed to the tremors, flashes, and claps of thunder.

"Yes, yes, I've experienced a supercell before," Mr. Debrid said. "They're certainly terrifying, but they're also beautiful. There aren't many times you see such brilliant lights come from the sky."

I could see the old man smile through his white beard as he looked out the window, contemplating the storm.

"Fifty years ago, I witnessed a supercell. Some believed it was the wrath of God coming from the sky. Others believed it was God making himself known by showing his power. And then there was another group.

They tried to explain the phenomenon with science, but no science could explain a storm like that one. It was supernatural."

Mr. Debrid looked me in the eye before continuing. His stare felt uncomfortable, like he was looking right through me. He knew that we came to him for more than just the history of supercells. He opened his mouth to speak, and I held my breath. I somehow knew what he was going to say.

His voice was gentle. "You lost a friend in the storm, didn't you?"

Anniyah, Lucas, and I looked at each other in shock.

"How did you know, Mr. Debrid?" Anniyah asked.

"Back during the series of supercells that took place when I was a child, I also lost a friend to the wild forces of the air. A bolt of lightning shot down from the sky and took my best friend right before my eyes. I watched as the lightning consumed his body. I saw the shadow of his skull—the light was so overwhelming that I could see his bones." He paused and shook his head. "But I couldn't believe that he was dead. There were just no signs of his death! I went to my parents, but they didn't believe me, so I went to the police. They didn't believe me, but they started a search for my friend anyway. It was no use. We never found him, and he was believed to have died or run away. Not even my friend's parents would believe me." Mr. Debrid looked down at his wrinkled hands and clutched them tightly, taking a moment to remember his friend.

I broke the silence. "So what did you do?"

"Well, I knew he was taken by the storm, so I assumed I had to face the storm to save him." Mr. Debrid lowered his voice. "You must be very brave if you wish to save your friend."

My friends and I looked at each other and nodded. We could do this.

"We're plenty brave, sir," Lucas said confidently.

"You will need to find the eye of the storm."

"The eye of the storm?" I parroted, unsure.

"Yes—that's where the center of the storm is. Your friend is trapped in a vortex that takes you to another realm."

Anniyah's eyes bulged. "You mean a whole other world?"

Mr. Debrid nodded and continued. "When your friend was struck by lightning, he was sent to another world and appeared in the vortex. But the vortex only opens during the storms. If the storms pass—"

"—Bryan will be trapped forever," I finished his sentence. It was all coming together. Bryan was trapped there, and we had to pull him out.

"Is that where you found your friend, Mr. Debrid?" Lucas asked.

Mr. Debrid dropped his head a little. "Yes, but I was too late. I saw my friend—his name was Sean. He was in the vortex all alone, frozen in the same position as when he was struck by lightning. I reached out to grab him, but it was already too late. The storm passed. I waited for the next storm to come, but that was the last supercell. Sean was gone."

"Well, what are you waiting for!?" Anniyah stood up. "The supercells are back. This is your chance to get Sean back! And I heard on the news that the storms this week should be the last of them. This might be our only chance!"

Mr. Debrid smiled and shook his head. "No, it's okay. I don't know if Sean's still out there or not. But I like to believe that he's in a better place. I can feel it. I know he's okay." He paused and looked at me. "But now is the time to save your friend. Don't lose to the storm like I once did. Be brave and face the trial before you. It won't be easy, but bravery and confidence in your actions will help you overcome the hardships you will soon face."

We all nodded at Mr. Debrid.

"So, what do we do?" Lucas asked. "How do we find the vortex and pull Bryan out?"

"The vortex will appear at the very center of the storm's core. You have to look at the clouds to find it. Search for the place where lightning seems to strike most frequently. That's how you'll know when you're close. Once you figure that out, your friend should be waiting there. Reach in and pull him out, but be quick about it. If the vortex shuts, you'll lose your opportunity. Now go! Don't waste any time. And don't make the same mistake I made all those years ago."

With that, Anniyah, Lucas, and I stood up, gathered our boards, and thanked Mr. Debrid for his knowledge, aid, and encouragement.

We stepped back out into the storm.

There was no way for us to know how much longer the supercell would last. Time was against us, but bravery was on our side. Rain fell, thunder boomed, lightning flashed, and the ground shook.

We were unfazed and ready to defy the storm.

It was time to save Bryan.

EPILOGUE

"Jay..." my cousin said suspiciously. "You swear you're not making any of this up?" Arilyn frowned.

I sighed. "Arilyn, I told you: this is all true!"

She shrugged. "Well, if you were making it up, it would mean you have a great imagination. It's a great story."

I smirked at her, swung my hammock back and forth a few times, and stared at the trees above me.

"So..." Arilyn started anxiously. "What happened next? Did you save Bryan?"

"Oh, so now you're interested?" I laughed, teasing her. "I thought you said I made this all up?"

"Okay, okay, sorry. I believe you." She grinned, grabbing the ropes of the hammock. "But don't leave me hanging here. Did you find the vortex?"

I smiled at her and leaned back in my hammock. At first, I hadn't wanted to tell her my story. I knew it'd be hard to believe. It was also full of emotions and haunting memories. But there was something about telling Arilyn the story that made my heart feel warm. I don't know if it was the feeling of learning to be brave in the face of danger, or if I'd just been out in the sun all day, and the bright rays trickling through the branches were getting to me. Either way, it felt good to finally tell someone my secret, summer adventure.

"Hellooooo? Earth to Jay! Are you gonna tell me or not?" Arilyn asked impatiently.

"Haha sorry—I was thinking," I admitted. "Okay, I'll tell you." I sat up in my hammock, hanging my legs over the side, and looked over at Arilyn. "Alright, so where were we?" I tapped my finger on my chin as I thought about where we'd left off. I looked down at the ground, hoping something would jog my memory. I saw my skateboard. "Ah, yes! We'd just left Frank's Ice Cream shop where Mr. Debrid had given us some advice, and—"

"I'm back with ice cream," I voice shouted from behind us.

I turned around and saw Chris, Arilyn's older brother, walking towards us.

"I guess the rest of the story will have to wait till next time," I said with a smile.

Arilyn scrunched up her nose, irritated at having to wait.

Chris handed each of us a cone. "So, what have you two been talking about?"

"Nothing!" we said in unison.

Chris looked back and forth at us and raised an eyebrow. "Oh yeah?"

"Uh, I was just telling Arilyn a story."

"I see. What was it about?" Chris asked.

"Well—" I paused to think about how to phrase my words without giving anything away. I grinned at Chris. "It's about overcoming tough times with bravery."

Chris smiled and went back to eating his ice cream. We ate in silence, enjoying the gentle breeze in Central Park. I caught a look from Arilyn, who seemed very eager to hear the rest of the story. I winked at her. She was going to have to wait until next time.

Made in the USA
Columbia, SC
19 July 2020